D1401026

# Steve Young

## NFL Passing Wizard

### by Bill Gutman

MILLBROOK SPORTS WORLD
THE MILLBROOK PRESS
BROOKFIELD, CONNECTICUT

Photographs courtesy of NFL Photos: cover (© Michael Zagaris), cover inset (© James D. Smith), pp. 8 (Young Family), 9 (Young Family), 11 (Steve Young) , 30 (Peter Reid Miller) , 44 (Paul Jasienski), 46 (Tony Tomsic); Wide World: pp. 3, 4, 19, 20, 23, 26-27, 32, 37, 40, 42; Mark A. Philbrick, Brigham Young University Sports Information: pp. 12, 14, 17, 21; Allsport: pp. 24 (Mike Powell), 28 (Otto Gruele), 34 (Mike Powell).

Library of Congress Cataloging-in-Publication Data
Gutman, Bill.
Steve Young : NFL passing wizard / by Bill Gutman.
p. cm. — (Millbrook sports world)
Summary: Covers the personal life and football career of the quarterback who played at Brigham Young University and with the San Francisco 49ers and was named Most Valuable Player in Superbowl XXIX in 1995.
ISBN 1-56294-184-4 (lib. bdg.)  ISBN 0-7613-0134-8 (pbk.)
1. Young, Steve, 1961–  —Juvenile literature. 2. Football players—United States—Bibliography—Juvenile literature. 3. San Francisco 49ers (Football team)—Juvenile Literature. [1. Young, Steve, 1961–  . 2. Football players.] I. Title. II Series.
GV939.Y69G88  1996
796.332'092—dc20  [B]  96-6420  CIP  AC

Published by The Millbrook Press, Inc.
2 Old New Milford Road
Brookfield, Connecticut 06804

# STEVE YOUNG

**W**hen the San Francisco 49ers came out onto the field at Joe Robbie Stadium in Miami on January 29, 1995, no one had to tell them it was the biggest game of the year. The San Diego Chargers players knew it, too. After all, the two teams were meeting in the Super Bowl, the game to determine the champion of the National Football League.

But for Steve Young, the 6-foot-2, 200-pound quarterback of the 49ers, this game was special. Although he had played in a lot of big games, there was more at stake in this one than ever before.

Steve Young was fighting to get out of a shadow, perhaps the biggest one a quarterback had ever cast. The shadow belonged to Joe Montana, who had

*Steve Young, ready to complete another pass downfield in Super Bowl XXIX. Steve threw his first touchdown pass to Jerry Rice on just the third play of the game. He would throw five more in a record-setting performance before the game ended.*

been San Francisco's quarterback before Steve. Montana had delivered four Super Bowl titles to the Bay Area and was called by many the greatest pro quarterback of all time.

When an elbow injury to Montana allowed Steve to take over the job in 1991, Steve proved to be an outstanding starting quarterback. But the ball club fell short of returning to the Super Bowl that year. The fans were rough on Steve. Joe could deliver championships, the fans said. Apparently, Steve could not. Despite the criticism, Steve continued to do what he had always done: Play the best he could while helping his team win football games. By 1994 the Niners were considered by many to be the best team in the league. The pressure was on to win the Super Bowl. And no one felt that pressure more than the team's tough left-handed quarterback.

The Niners won the coin toss and ran the kickoff back to their own 41-yard line. Steve led the Niner offense onto the field. His first play was a simple handoff to fullback William Floyd. This allowed everyone a play to get the feel of the game and do some hitting. Floyd gained four yards.

Then, on second down, Steve dropped back for his first pass. He whipped the ball to wide receiver John Taylor for an 11-yard gain and a first down. Now the Niners were in San Diego territory at the 44-yard line.

Once again, Steve barked the signals. He took the snap from center, faked a handoff to halfback Ricky Watters, then dropped back again. As he did, All-Pro wide receiver Jerry Rice bolted straight downfield for a few yards, faked to the outside, then cut back to the inside on a post pattern. As Rice made his cut inside, Steve Young cranked his left arm and threw the ball to the place he knew Rice would be when the ball got there.

Sure enough, the speedy Rice grabbed the perfect pass in full stride and raced into the clear. He was gone, running into the end zone to complete a 44-yard touchdown play. A smiling Steve Young raced downfield to congratulate his receiver. The Niners had scored after just 84 seconds. Steve could feel it already: This was going to be his day.

## EARLY SKILLS

Great athletes don't always make great quarterbacks. In the case of Steve Young, it wasn't until he was well into his college career that he began to show the passing skills that would take him to the National Football League. Before that he was known more for his running than for his throwing.

Jon Steven Young was born in Salt Lake City, Utah, on October 11, 1961. He was the oldest of four boys born to LeGrande and Sherry Young, both of whom were Mormons. Salt Lake City is the center of the Mormon faith, having been established in 1847 after the Mormons were driven from the East by religious persecution.

In fact, the Young family is directly related to Mormon leader Brigham Young, after whom Brigham Young University in Provo, Utah, is named. Steve and his brothers are the great-great-great grandsons of Brigham Young. His father attended Brigham Young and played football in 1954, 1958, and 1959. A fullback and linebacker, LeGrande Young led the team in total offense with 423 rushing yards in 1959.

But the Youngs did not remain in Salt Lake City for long. LeGrande Young took his family across the country and settled in Greenwich, Connecticut, a prosperous community just 45 minutes from New York City. There, Mr. Young began practicing law and helping to raise his growing family.

Because he had been a good athlete himself, LeGrande Young watched his first son carefully. He began seeing some unusual qualities in Steve very early. Between two and three years of age, Steve could already do pushups and dribble a basketball.

*Even when he relaxed at home, sports were never far from Steve's mind. It must have been baseball season when this photo was taken, since Steve is wearing the uniform of his junior high team.*

"It was pretty obvious to me he [Steve] had some gifts," Mr. Young said. "He was a very tenacious kid . . . I'd say more than most kids."

When LeGrande Young had played football, he nickname was "Grit," and that's what he saw in Steve as his son grew and began to play baseball, basketball, and football. Even as a kid, Steve had a burning desire to excel and win. And he expected those playing alongside him to put forth the same kind of effort he did, game after game.

Sports played a big part in Steve's life right through elementary school and junior high. He played on Little League, town, and school teams and always did well. At the same time, his parents made sure he didn't neglect his schoolwork. Steve applied his work ethic to his studies and was a top student as well as a top athlete.

## A STAR QUARTERBACK WITHOUT A PASSING ARM

At Greenwich High School, Steve began making a reputation as a star athlete. He excelled at football, baseball, and basketball. As much as having solid skills then, his stubborn refusal to lose was what made him special.

Steve took over as the starting quarterback his junior year and played each game as if his life depended on it. When he didn't hand the ball off, he took it around one end or the other, and sometimes even off-tackle, something quarterbacks normally don't do.

Fast and strong, Steve was completely fearless when he ran the ball. He would put his head down and battle for every extra yard. When he threw, however, it wasn't pretty. He wasn't an accurate passer, and the ball often fluttered in the air. So Coach Mike Ornato worked to his quarterback's strength. He had a fine blocking team that paved the way for Steve's runs.

*At Greenwich High School, Steve was a rollout quarterback who almost always ran the ball. His few passes wobbled and fluttered. But when he took off, he was hard to stop.*

By the time he was a senior in 1979, Greenwich High had an outstanding team. Steve was the co-captain and the leader. His teammates respected him and looked to him to get the job done. They didn't mind that he was the one who usually got the headlines.

"One thing about Steve, he was alway a down-to-earth guy," his high school teammate Mike Gasparino once said. "[He was] a true friend. You never begrudged him anything. To see him succeed, everyone wanted to see that. [Because] he was always the type of guy who deserved everything he got."

Late in the season a number of college scouts were looking at Steve. But none were scouting him as a quarterback. It was his running that attracted them. In fact, during one game Steve was moved to halfback for several series just to showcase his running.

The first play designed for Steve that day called for him to run off right tackle. With his usual solid blocking, Steve burst through a hole, faked a linebacker, cut back outside and raced 75 yards for a touchdown.

"I get a kick when I hear people say he shouldn't run so much," Coach Ornato said.

In other words, it's best to stick with a winning formula, and Greenwich was winning with Steve running the football. He took the team all the way to the county championship game against rival Darien High School. Darien clearly had the better team, and by the fourth quarter it was apparent they would win.

But Steve wouldn't quit. He kept urging his teammates to keep plugging, for one more play, one more yard, one more first down. As co-captain Mike Gasparino recalled: "The sound in his voice, you could tell it was coming from the heart. All game, we would do the blocking, but it was pretty much all him. He brought us farther than we ever should have gone. . . . Even though the game was pretty much over, he was still pushing us."

Steve carried the football some 275 times in his two varsity seasons at Greenwich. Those are running back numbers, not the usual rushing workload for a quarterback. He rarely passed. Yet he became an honorable mention Prep All-American and was an obvious All-County choice.

But he contributed even more than that. He went on to be a captain of both the basketball and baseball teams. As a senior he averaged 20 points a game in basketball and hit .600 with the baseball team. His grades were so good that he became a member of the school's Honor Society and was a National Merit Scholarship nominee.

It was no surprise that Steve was actively recruited by a number of fine schools. Because of his Mormon affiliation and because his father had gone there, Steve decided to attend Brigham Young University, at Provo. He would enter in the fall of 1980 and be joining a Cougar team renowned for something that Steve hadn't done much: passing the football.

*Steve was an all-around athlete at Greenwich High. When he wasn't starring on the gridiron or batting .600 on the diamond, he was averaging 20 points a game on the basketball court.*

# *FOLLOWING A TRADITION*

The Brigham Young Cougars under coach LaVell Edwards always threw the football. In fact, the team used a pro-type offense that featured a passing quarterback. Because of that, the school had a tradition of developing quarterbacks who moved on to play in the National Football League.

When Steve entered college as a freshman, the starting quarterback was Jim McMahon, who was not only a record-setter at BYU, but would go on to lead the Chicago Bears to a Super Bowl triumph five years later.

*As a freshman at Brigham Young University, Steve scored more in the classroom than on the football field. Although he wasn't a good enough player to make the varsity team, his grades were always high.*

The first time Steve looked at the team's depth chart he was listed as the eighth quarterback on the list, meaning that seven other quarterbacks were rated higher. He was, in effect, eighth string.

In fact, Steve wasn't even good enough to make the varsity that year. He became one of the quarterbacks on the Junior Varsity squad and did many of the same things he had done in high school. In other words, he ran a lot more than he passed.

But there was no chance that the BYU varsity would even consider a run-oriented offense. In fact, after the season Steve learned that the coaches thought so little of his passing skills that they were thinking of making him a defensive back. The news stunned Steve. He was so upset that he even considered leaving school.

"I called home and told my folks I was quitting school and heading back to Connecticut," Steve related. "But Dad got on the phone and said if I did come back, I couldn't live at home. 'There are no quitters living here,' Dad told me, and that settled that."

So Steve stayed at BYU even though his football future was in doubt. Then in January 1981, BYU changed assistant coaches, and the move changed Steve's football career.

Ted Tollner was the new quarterback coach. "I was throwing in the indoor facility just after Coach Tollner signed on," Steve said, "and he made it a point to report to Coach Edwards that I should be given a chance to throw in spring ball."

It wasn't that Steve couldn't throw the football. He had a strong throwing arm. And once he began working to develop it, he found that he could be accurate as well. He could put the ball on the mark.

During spring practice, the coaches couldn't get over the progress he had made. He quickly began moving up the depth chart. By the time the 1981

season was set to open, Steve was up to the number two slot. He was the backup behind All-American Jim McMahon.

"I think the amazing thing about Steve is that he had come farther quicker than anybody I've seen," Coach Edwards said. "He came out of a prep program where they didn't throw the ball much, and he had to learn a passing system which is pretty complicated. He simply went out and did it."

The Cougars opened the 1981 season with McMahon at the helm. As usual, the team had a big-yardage passing attack and scored a lot of points. With substantial leads in all of the first three games, Steve got a chance at his first taste of varsity action, throwing a few passes in each. The team was winning big. Then, in the following week against Colorado, the unexpected happened.

McMahon suffered a knee injury early in the second half, and Steve had to come on. This would be his first sustained piece of action. Even though the Cougars were leading, Steve knew the game was still up for grabs. He had to perform.

He completed just four of ten passes for 63 yards, but two of them went for touchdowns. Even more impressive were his four runs out of the backfield for 61 yards. He could still run the football as well as most running backs. BYU won the game, and Steve felt what it was like to win in the big time.

Then the news came that McMahon would probably be out at least two weeks. With Utah State as the next opponent, Steve Young was suddenly the Cougars starter. For a quarterback who had been considered a passing dud

*Steve's passing improved rapidly. By 1981 he was the backup to starter Jim McMahon. He could stay in the pocket and throw, but if rushed he could scamper away and run like a halfback.*

just a year earlier, Steve put on quite a show. He completed 21 of 40 passes for 307 yards and a score. In addition, he carried the ball 21 times for 63 rushing yards. BYU won the game, 32-26, to remain unbeaten.

A week later he did another solid job against Nevada-Las Vegas, although four of his passes were intercepted. But it was the defense that didn't hold up and UNLV scored in the final seconds to win it, 45-41. That snapped a 17-game BYU win streak. Yet there was only praise for Steve Young, who had played like a seasoned veteran.

McMahon returned the following week, and Steve threw just one pass the rest of the season. He wound up with 56 completions in 112 tries for 731 yards, hitting at a 50 percent clip. He threw for five scores and had five picked off. Not bad for a guy who had been eighth string a year earlier.

Off the field, Steve continued to study hard. He had a double major in accounting and international relations. After the season, he was named to the All-Academic team of the Western Athletic Conference (WAC).

With McMahon's career ending, Steve would be returning in 1982 as the number one quarterback and the first left-handed thrower in Brigham Young University's history.

## CONSENSUS ALL-AMERICAN

In the first game of the 1982 season against Nevada-Las Vegas, Steve completed 19 of 26 passes for 271 yards and a touchdown, as BYU won easily. But a week later, the Cougars were beaten by Georgia. Steve hit just 22 of 46 throws, and to make matters worse, he threw six interceptions.

In the next game, the team lost again, beaten by the Air Force Academy before 66,000 home fans. Everyone was disheartened, especially Steve.

*With McMahon gone, Steve took over as the number-one quarterback in 1982. He commanded respect in the huddle and produced a fine season, leading the Cougars to a seventh straight conference title and becoming WAC Offensive Player of the Year.*

"There were times when I questioned myself in those early games," Steve would admit later. "But I convinced myself that a throwing football team will make mistakes and that I had to keep plugging away."

Perhaps it was the game against Texas-El Paso the following week that gave Steve the shot-in-the-arm he needed. It was the first huge game of his career. He connected on 24 of 32 passes for 399 yards and two scores, and rushed for 97 yards on just 13 carries as the Cougars won easily. He had generated 496 yards of total offense all by himself.

From there, BYU cruised to six straight WAC victories and its seventh straight conference title. Steve Young had put together a truly fine season as starting quarterback. In 11 games, he completed 230 of 367 passes for an outstanding 62.7 percentage. He threw for 3,100 yards and had 18 touchdowns and 18 intercepts. He also ran for 407 yards on 114 carries.

Steve had become the accurate passer he had dreamed of being, setting an NCAA record by completing 22 successive passes at one point in the season. He was named WAC Offensive Player of the Year and a District Seven Academic All-American.

Many people were predicting big things for him in 1983, and Steve was determined not to disappoint them. He worked harder than ever.

"I love practice," he told a reporter. "I can't wait to go back out each day. It never gets monotonous. It's a constant challenge. This game is fun and I intend to keep it that way. As long as I work hard to improve, I think my game will keep improving."

Steve's work ethic began to pay off. In the opening game of the 1983 season, he was nearly a one-man wrecking crew for the Cougar offense even though the team was beaten. More confident than ever, he hit on 23 of 38 passes for 351 yards and a touchdown. In addition, he ran for 113 yards on 13 carries, an average of more than 10 yards a pop.

*Steve was a passing wizard in his senior year at Brigham Young. Yet he was still a great runner as well. Here he breaks several Baylor tackles as he heads for a touchdown in a Cougar victory over the Bears.*

*In the season finale against Utah, Steve threw for six touchdowns in a 55-7 victory and set six NCAA records in the process. He was a consensus All-American and had the most famous left arm in college football.*

Steve went on to lead the Cougars to one victory after another. Against the Air Force he hit on 39 of 49 passes for 486 yards and three scores. In a game against San Diego State he completed 32 of 45 for 446 yards and three TDs. And in the season finale against Utah he connected on 22 of 25 for 268 yards and an amazing six touchdowns!

"They [the coaches] don't put the chains on me to keep me from running," Steve said, during the season. "But the thrust of our offense is passing. I find passing a great challenge and have to work hard...every day to improve."

When the 1983 season ended the Cougars were 10-1 and the ninth-ranked team in the country. Steve had thrown for more than 300 yards in all but two games and topped the 400-yard mark twice. And after the season he became a consensus All-American and multi-time record setter.

"Steve came from virtually nowhere to where he's one of the most totally dominating players you'll ever see," Coach Edwards said, and the numbers bore that out. For the regular season, Steve completed 306 passes in 429 attempts for 3,902 yards and 33 touchdowns. His completion percentage was an outstanding 71.3, and he was intercepted just 10 times. In addition, he ran for another 444 yards in 102 carries and generated 4,346 yards in total offense for the season.

As for records, Steve set or tied 13 NCAA marks—nine for passing and four for total offense. Included among them were new standards for most total offense per game (395.1 yards), most 300-yard passing games in a career (18), most passes completed in a season (306), the highest completion percentage for a season and career (71.3 and 65.2), and most consecutive games throwing a touchdown pass (22). Many have since been broken in an increasingly pass-oriented sport. But Steve's accomplishments were nevertheless superb.

He finished his career by leading Brigham Young past Missouri, 21-17, in the Holiday Bowl and was named Player of the Game. In addition to becoming a consensus All-American, Steve was runner-up to running back Mike Rozier of

*Steve graduated from Brigham Young in May 1984. Standing before a statue of the school's founder (and a distant relative), he was just as proud of this uniform as the one he wore on the football field.*

Nebraska for the Heisman Trophy, given to the best college player in the land. His 3.38 grade-point average earned him second-team Academic All-America selection. He was a Football Foundation Hall of Fame Scholar-Athlete and received the NCAA "Top Five" Award, also given to scholar athletes.

Steve graduated with his class in May 1984. There was still a question about the future. He had talked of going to law school, but he was also considered the best college quarterback in the country. That usually led to playing in the National Football League.

But that year, there was another option besides the NFL. The new United States Football League was in operation and trying to compete with the NFL by playing its schedule in the spring. Steve didn't rule that out.

"Whatever comes will come," was the way he put it. "In pro ball, it's not so much the location as the organization you play for. I want to play for a top-notch organization."

## TRAVELIN' PRO QUARTERBACK

When the United States Football League held its draft early in 1984, Steve Young became the first-round pick (10th overall) of the Los Angeles Express. He wanted to make sure he completed his studies at BYU first. So he missed the first six games of the 1984 USFL season, then signed an incredible, multiyear contract worth a total of $40 million.

The USFL figured it had grabbed a real marquee player, a potential superstar and league spokesman. But it turned out to be the worst decision that Steve ever made. The league wasn't nearly as good as the NFL. One team, in fact, played on a dirt field in a junior college stadium.

Steve played 12 games for the Express in 1984 and 13 in the spring of 1985. He played well enough, but didn't really show the skills to be a top QB in the National Football League. By that time, the USFL was in serious financial trouble (and would cease operations prior to the 1986 season). Some teams wanted to rid themselves of big contracts. So Steve was released and didn't get most of the money in his huge contract.

Then, in early September, Steve signed with the Tampa Bay Buccaneers of the National Football League. The Bucs had the rights to him from the 1984 NFL supplemental draft of USFL players. He would finally get a chance to play with the best.

"I knew I didn't have a good year with L.A.," Steve said. "But hard work had always enabled me to turn the corner before. That's what I hoped would

*Steve never really hit his stride in the struggling USFL. But he still had his running ability. Here he eludes tackles by Chicago Blitz defenders in a 1984 game.*

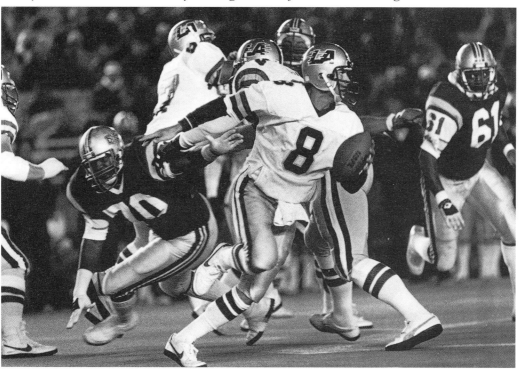

*After two years with Tampa Bay, Steve was traded to the San Francisco 49ers prior to the 1987 season. The Niners were quarterbacked by Joe Montana, shown here.*

happen with Tampa Bay." It turned out to be more of a struggle than he expected.

Steve got to start five games with Tampa Bay in the fall of 1985. He completed just 52.2 percent of his passes, threw for three scores but had eight interceptions. His quarterback rating was a low 56.9. It looked as if he was coming to a crossroads in his career.

It didn't help that he was playing for a team that went 2-14 for the season. And things didn't look much better for the Bucs in 1986. Steve won the starting quarterback job in the preseason and hoped to do better than in the previous year. The problem was that he would once again be playing for a team that would go 2-14. It's difficult for any player to excel in that kind of losing situation.

So once again Steve failed to put up numbers that would indicate a coming star quarterback. In 14 games, Steve could do no better than a 65.5 QB rating. He had 8 TD throws but 13 interceptions. And he completed just 53.7 percent of his passes.

Steve wasn't used to losing teams, or failure. But then things changed unexpectedly. Four days before the 1987 NFL draft was set to be held in April, Steve learned he had been traded to the San Francisco 49ers.

It was as if he had gone from the basement to the penthouse. The Niners had won the Super Bowl for the 1981 and 1984 seasons. And they had a powerful team that could do it again. The team had been 10-5-1 in 1986 before losing in the playoffs. That was the good news.

The bad news was that the Niners had one of the game's leading quarterbacks. Joe Montana had directed the team since 1979 and was the architect of both Super Bowl victories. Known as the Comeback Kid for his late-game heroics, Montana was on his way to becoming an all-time great. Steve was being brought in strictly as a backup.

It was also his third pro team in three years. He began to wonder if he would ever again achieve the success he had tasted as a collegian.

## FROM BACKUP TO NUMBER ONE

Someone once said that Steve Young's handsome face was not the face of a backup quarterback. Of course, that might not have been said if Steve hadn't had a world of talent. But the truth was that by 1987, many football fans were beginning to think of Steve as little more than a solid backup quarterback.

With the 49ers, Steve knew he would have to be ready to take over if Montana got hurt. Leading a team that featured star wide receivers Jerry Rice and John Taylor, a good running game, and a strong offensive line was a luxury he had never had before.

Unfortunately, Steve didn't see much playing time. For a competitor like Steve, sitting the bench wasn't easy. In 1987 he started three games when Montana was hurt and played in parts of five others. In the other eight games, he sat. But he also made the most of his opportunities.

Against New Orleans he completed five of six passes, including a 46-yard TD strike to Jerry Rice. When Montana went down with a hamstring pull against the Bears, Steve came on and threw four touchdown passes.

For the season, he completed 37 of 69 throws for 570 yards. Amazingly, he threw for 10 touchdowns without a single interception. His quarterback rating for the year was 120.8. Had he been a regular, that would have been a record. Although Steve was just a backup, he showed quickly that he was among the best in the league.

The Niners finished the 1987 season with a 13-2 record, winning their division. But in the NFC Playoff game, they were upset by Minnesota, 36-24. Steve replaced Montana in the third quarter, completed 12 of 17 passes for 158

*Playing for the injured Montana in a December 1987 game against the Chicago Bears, Steve surprised everyone by throwing four touchdown passes. And he hadn't forgotten how to run. Here he dives to the one-yard line against the tough Chicago defense.*

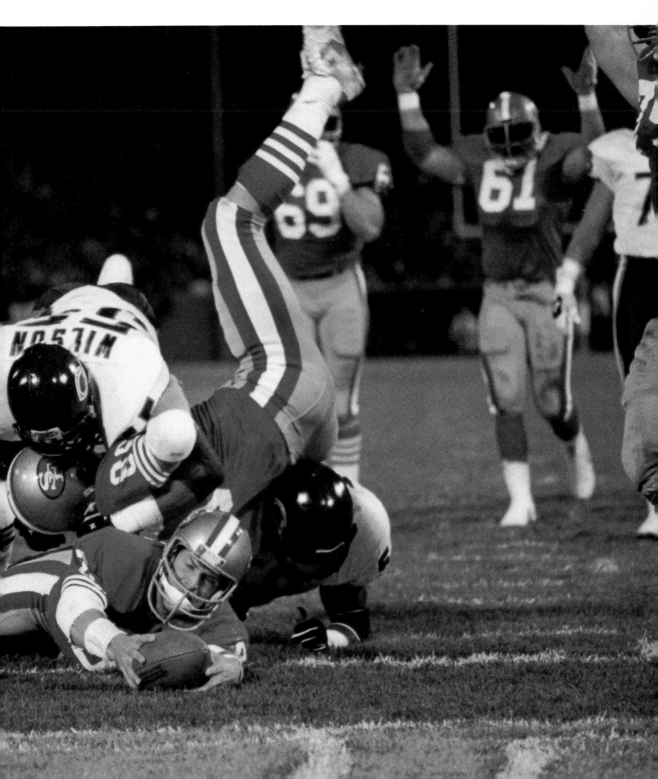

*An elbow injury to Montana allowed Steve to finally become the starting quarterback in 1991. Soon NFL defenses were seeing the same thing that teams playing Brigham Young had seen: a dangerous quarterback with an accurate passing arm and the ability to scramble and run.*

yards and rushed for 72 yards on just six carries. He had played very well, but it was a Vikings day.

It was more of the same for the next three seasons. In January 1989, Montana led the Niners to yet another Super Bowl triumph as the club topped Cincinnati, 20-16, in the championship game. Montana completed 23 of 36 passes for 357 yards and two touchdowns in that game. At age 32, he was heralded as the best in the game and one of the best ever.

Steve had very little chance of taking Montana's job. He started just three games and played in 11, throwing just 101 passes and three touchdowns. A year later, in 1990, the Niners won a fourth Super Bowl after a 14-2 regular season. Montana was again the star as his club whipped Denver, 55-10, in the super game. This time Montana set a Super Bowl record by throwing for five touchdowns. Steve Young had two Super Bowl rings, but was still a backup.

Steve had thrown for 1,001 yards in the regular season and once again had an impressive 120.8 quarterback rating. But he attempted just 92 passes all year. And in 1990 he tossed just 62, starting only one game as Montana compiled 3,944 yards with 26 TDs. Joe won the NFL passing title and was now being called by many the best quarterback ever to play the game.

But in the playoffs following the 1990 season, the Niners were edged in the NFC title game by the New York Giants, 15-13. Otherwise, they would have gone to yet another Super Bowl. Again, Steve watched. But how long could the fiercely competitive Young sit the bench?

Then, in 1991, fate took a hand. Before the season started, it was revealed that Joe Montana had a serious elbow injury, which would require surgery. The word was that the injury would not only keep Super Joe out all season, but it might end his career. Suddenly, without much warning, Steve Young was *the* quarterback of the 49ers.

As usual, Steve said the right things. "Everyone wants the best for Joe and hopes he gets back as soon as possible," he said. "Until then, we're all going to do our best to carry on the tradition."

That tradition was winning. The Super Bowl was an annual goal for a team that had already won it four times since the 1981 season. So Steve stepped in, and with that same strong cast of characters around him, showed that he was more than ready to take over the leadership of the offense.

In his first start against the Giants, he tossed a 73-yard touchdown pass, proving he had the arm to go deep. A week later against San Diego, he completed 26 of 36 for a whopping 348 yards and three scores. He had superior accuracy, too, as well as a feel for the complex passing game of the 49ers. In a game against Atlanta he was on fire to the tune of another 348 passing yards. He was named NFC Player of the Week for that one.

A week later against Detroit, he set a 49ers record by hitting on 18 of 20 passes for a 90 percent accuracy mark. He was named *USA Today* Player of the Week after that game. There was little doubt now that Steve was ready for prime time. He was doing it all.

Unfortunately, Steve's season was derailed when he injured a knee in the tenth game against Atlanta. He then missed five straight games and most of a sixth. He didn't return full time until the final game of the year, against the Chicago Bears. But not even the forced layoff hurt him, as he completed 21 of 32 passes for 338 yards and three touchdowns.

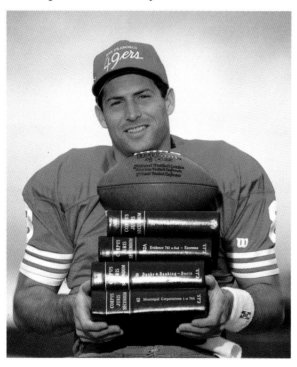

*Always looking toward the future, Steve returned to Brigham Young in the off-season to study law. Football was still number one, but now Steve was balancing his life with law books. Not many athletes could carry that kind of load.*

The problem was that the Niners finished the season with a 10-6 record, not good enough to make the playoffs. *If we only had Joe in the lineup*, many fans lamented. They were referring, of course, to the absent Montana. But Steve had certainly made his own mark.

He finished the year with 180 completions in 279 tries, a 64.5 completions percentage. In addition, he threw for 2,517 yards with 17 touchdowns and just 8 interceptions. His quarterback rating of 101.8 was the best in the National Football League.

No one could deny that Steve Young had arrived.

# OUT FROM THE SHADOW

In a way, Steve Young's career was just taking off. But even then Steve knew he couldn't play football forever. During the off-season he continued to return to Brigham Young where he studied law at the J. Reuben Clark Law School—not an easy task for someone who had to concentrate on football for a good part of the year.

He was also becoming involved in charitable activities. He had founded the Forever Young Charity Foundation, which benefits Bay Area and Utah youth-oriented charities. He worked on behalf of children with disabilities, serving as honorary chariman for the Children's Miracle Network in San Francisco. He was also a spokesman for the Contra Costa Sheriff's Office Anti-Drug campaign. In addition, he was a frequent speaker at church, community, and charity functions throughout the country. He gave whatever time he had available.

On the football front, there was bad news for 49ers fans before the 1992 season. Joe Montana's elbow still wasn't healed enough for him to play. The word was that he would be out for most of the year. The good news was that the team had a healthy Steve Young to take his place.

"I was happy for Joe when he was doing well," said Niners Coach George Seifert. "But this city has been so lucky. Joe Montana, followed by Steve Young. People don't understand that that doesn't happen."

Seifert meant that to go from one great quarterback right to another is highly unusual. But in the eyes of many 49ers fans, Steve was still a caretaker quarterback, doing the job *only* until Montana returned.

In the second week of the season, Steve had one of his stellar games, completing 26 of 37 passes against Buffalo, good for 449 yards and three TDs. He was on his way. From there, he went on to produce his best season yet, leading the Niners to a league-best 14-2 record and topping the league in a number of passing categories.

He completed 268 of 402 passes for 3,465 yards, a 66.7 completion percentage, 25 touchdowns and only 7 intercepts. His 107.0 quarterback rating was by far the best in the league. He also was first in completion percentage and TD passes. And he became the first NFL quarterback to lead the league two straight seasons with a rating of 100 or better.

*With Montana still injured, Steve produced a brilliant season in 1992 and was the NFL passing champ. Here he gives a thumbs up after being named NFL Player of the Year. He was also the league's Most Valuable Player.*

That was only the beginning. He was named an All-Pro, was the *Sports Illustrated*, Miller Lite, and *Sporting News* Player of the Year, and won the Len Eshmont Award as the team's most inspirational and courageous player in a vote of his teammates. And then, to top it all off, he was named the NFL's Most Valuable Player!

That still wasn't enough for the fans. They were more excited by the return of Joe Montana in the final game of the season. Joe played just briefly and looked good, tossing a touchdown pass. The Legend was back.

But that didn't mean Joe would be handed the QB job for the playoffs. No coach would bench the league's Most Valuable Player. So Steve was at the helm when the Niners met the Washington Redskins in their first post-season game. Steve tossed a pair of TD's in the first half and led his team to a 20-13 victory. He completed 20 of 30 passes for 227 yards.

"It was a relief, a thrill, a little of both," he said. "Around here, playoff wins are kind of the norm."

Then, in the NFC title game, the Niners hosted the powerful Dallas Cowboys at Candlestick Park. These were considered the two best teams in pro football. The winner would be a heavy favorite to win the Super Bowl. The Cowboys were loaded on both offense and defense. Beating them wouldn't be easy.

The two powerhouses were evenly matched. Dallas finally opened it up in the fourth quarter to win, 30-20. Steve played well, but his Dallas counterpart Troy Aikman had played better. The Niners were out, and some said it wouldn't have been that way with Montana as the quarterback.

As one writer put it, "No matter what they say, no matter what he does short of four Super Bowl championships, it will never be Steve Young's team. It will forever be Joe Montana's team."

Then prior to the 1993 season, there was a big change. The team had to decide between the two quarterbacks. Neither would relish being a backup, so the club's management traded the older Montana to the Kansas City Chiefs. Now Steve wouldn't have the Legend looking over his shoulder.

But the 1993 season was, in a way, more of the same. Steve had an outstanding regular season. He set an NFL record by winning three straight passing titles and became the only quarterback in league history to have three straight seasons with a 100-plus quarterback rating. He also became the first 49ers QB to throw for more than 4,000 yards (4,023) and set another team record by throwing 183 passes without an interception. The Niners won their division once more, but this time with a 10-6 record. Although they were the highest-scoring team in the league, the defense didn't play as well as they had in the past.

Now came the crucial playoffs. Once again the pressure was on Steve to win a Super Bowl. In the divisional playoff game, the Niners buried the New York Giants, 44-3, with Steve hitting on 17 of 25 passes for 226 yards. But next came the defending Super Bowl champ Dallas Cowboys again. The teams would meet in Dallas in the NFC title game to determine who would go to the Super Bowl.

This time the Cowboys really dominated. They sacked Steve four times, and knocked him down seven more. They also stopped receiver Jerry Rice and running back Ricky Watters. When it ended, Dallas had a 38-21 victory, and the Niners had to be asking what they could do to win.

*Steve threw for more than 4,000 yards in 1993 and won his third straight league passing title. But because the Niners lost to Dallas in the NFC title game, critics said he couldn't take the team to the Super Bowl.*

Steve and his teammates were frustrated. "We just needed a couple of stops early so we could get into the flow and get some work done," he said. "But it didn't happen and we started to play catchup. I would never have believed that we would come down here and get beat like this. But we'll just have to battle back and earn the right to do this again."

Back in San Francisco, the fans still tended to point fingers at the quarterback. Dallas won a second straight Super Bowl. Many just didn't believe Steve Young would ever win one.

## SUPER STEVE AT LAST

Despite three notable seasons, Steve was again on the hot seat when the 1994 season began. As offensive tackle Steve Wallace said, "The fans hated him because he was replacing a legend [Montana]."

None of it made sense. Except for not winning a Super Bowl, Steve had been brilliant. He remained quiet about the criticism for the most part, but in 1994 finally began to speak out. Commenting on the verbal abuse he had endured from the fans, he said: "I wouldn't have wished it on anybody. It was hard to be rational about it. Because it wasn't rational. And at the time, I thought, 'This is not fun. This hurts. This is not deserved.' But I wasn't going to let my life be dragged down to the point where I hated going to work."

Steve didn't let it affect his life. He had continued attending law school in the off-season and earned his degree. Not a bad thing to add to a resume that already read NFL Most Valuable Player and All-Pro. But none of that mattered when the 1994 season started. Only winning did.

The club had won three of its first four games, with Steve averaging nearly 300 yards passing. He had already thrown for nine touchdowns when the club hosted the Philadelphia Eagles in their fifth game. Suddenly, nothing was going right. Steve was having one of the poorest days of his career, and his teammates were not doing much better.

Late in the game the Eagles had a 40-8 lead. That's when Coach Seifert signaled Steve out of the game. When he reached the sidelines, the usually reserved Young began screaming at his coach. The two were going jaw to jaw, something that had never happened before. Everyone saw it. The Eagles won the game, but Steve's outburst seemed to trigger something in the Niners that hadn't been seen before.

"The coach told me I was getting beat up," Steve said, later. "But I was embarrassed by [being removed]. I was screaming at anybody who would

*Steve and the Niners' All-Pro wide receiver Jerry Rice were a great passing combination. Both set 1994 records as the Niners finished the season with a league-best 13-3 record.*

listen. I said I was tired of taking this stuff, too easy a scapegoat. . . . I refused to take it [the blame] from that point on. Somebody was going to join me."

The next day it was the coach who apologized to his quarterback. "Steve took on the head coach and became one of the guys," Seifert said. "For whatever reason, the players seemed to embrace him more following that incident than anything else that's happened here. That then allowed him to become more free in his play."

The coach was right. Even though he had been brilliant for the previous three years, on that day Steve took over the team and became its leader, in both ability and spirit.

After Steve's outburst, the Niners rolled. They would lose only one more game all year. The team dominated its opponents nearly every week, and Young was putting together the greatest season of his career. . .and one of the best that any quarterback ever had.

Only the final numbers are needed here. The Niners finished with a league-best 13-3 record and another division title. Steve completed 324 of 461 passes for 3,969 yards, a league best and 49ers record completion rate of 70.3 percent. He set a club mark with 35 touchdown passes, with only 10 interceptions, and set a new NFL all-time record with a quarterback rating of 112.8.

In addition, he extended his record by winning a fourth straight NFL passing title. It was also a record fourth straight year with a QB rating of 100 or better. And his 96.8 career rating made him the highest-rated passer in NFL history to that point. Soon after, Steve was named the NFL's Most Valuable Player for the second time in three years.

The Niners were the favorites to win the Super Bowl. So Steve Young had one more mountain to climb. It started with an easy 44-15 divisional win over the Chicago Bears. Now, for the third straight year, the Niners had to meet the Dallas Cowboys in the NFC title game, with the winner going to the Super Bowl.

It was a game in which the ball bounced the right way for the Niners. Within the first seven minutes, the Niners converted three Cowboys turnovers into a 21-0 lead. Dallas fought back and closed the margin to 24-14 before halftime. But Steve and Jerry Rice teamed up on a 28-yard scoring aerial with eight seconds left in the half to make it 31-14. From there, the Niners rolled to a 38-28 victory. They had finally whipped the Cowboys and would be returning to the Super Bowl to meet the San Diego Chargers.

This time fan reaction was different. The Candlestick throng were cheering "Steve, Steve, Steve" even before the game ended. It must have been music to his ears.

"The Cowboys represented to us and to me roadblocks in the past," Steve said. "We had to get over them. . . . It's a great feeling you just can't believe, 47 guys coming together."

Steve and his teammates faced one more obstacle: Super Bowl XXIX at Joe Robbie Stadium in Miami. It was as if Steve had waited all his life for this moment. He wasn't about to let it go. It started on the opening drive of the game when he hit Jerry Rice with that 44-yard TD toss. Just minutes later, Steve led his club 79 yards on four plays, this time connecting with Watters on a 51-yard touchdown pass.

Two more touchdown passes from Steve's left arm made it a 28-10 game by the half. After that, it was a matter of playing it out. The Chargers didn't quit, but were no match for the all-around skills of the Niners. And Steve Young.

When it ended, San Francisco had won the game, 49-26, a record fifth Super Bowl win. But it was the first as a starter for Steve, who had hit on 24

of 36 passes for 325 yards and a Super Bowl record six touchdowns! The old record of five was held by Joe Montana.

Steve was elated. When the game ended, Steve took a victory lap around Candlestick Park, high-fiving fans along the way. And it was no surprise when he was named the game's Most Valuable Player. It ended his greatest year in the greatest of ways.

"It had to be this way today," he said. "Because otherwise people wouldn't have given us our due for the team we are. But they saw today. We put ourselves apart from the field today. We put some distance between us and the rest of the league."

There was no doubt that Steve was proud of his team. And they were proud of him, as well.

"The amount of pressure on the guy was unbelievable," said teammate Harris Barton. "The whole world tuned in to watch him fall on his face, and he threw six touchdown passes. It was great for him."

Another teammate, Jesse Sapolu, put it this way: "We were looking to show the fans that this was one of the great quarterbacks to ever play the game. At this point, no one can dispute that he had the best single season any quarterback ever had. He's one of the few guys you were so happy for. I mean truly, truly happy for him."

Most people felt that way about Steve. In an age when some athletes don't always present a wholesome image, Steve Young continues to be the

*After leading the Niners to the NFC title over the rival Cowboys, Steve played a brilliant Super Bowl game. He threw for a record six touchdowns, ran like a demon, and was the MVP as his team won the title, 49-26, over the San Diego Chargers.*

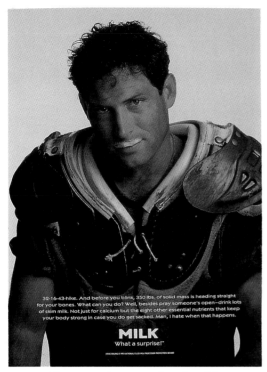

32-16-43-hike. And before you blink, 350 lbs. of solid mass is heading straight for your bones. What can you do? Well, besides pray someone's open—drink lots of skim milk. Not just for calcium but the eight other essential nutrients that keep your body strong in case you do get sacked. Man, I hate when that happens.

**MILK**
What a surprise!™

*Always a clean-cut, hardworking athlete, Steve lent his name and image to this advertisement for the benefits of drinking milk. With all he's accomplished in his life, no one is about to make fun of his choices.*

"boy next door." Despite the pressure of replacing Montana and trying to win a Super Bowl, Steve managed to finish law school and earn a degree.

After the Super Bowl, he flew to New York to be photographed for the dairy industry's "celebrity milk drinkers" campaign. (This was nothing new. He once chugged a mug of milk in high school when many of his teammates were chugging beer.)

It would be hard for Steve and his teammates to top the 1994 storybook season. They tried in 1995 but fell short, winning their division with an 11-5 mark, then losing to the Green Bay Packers in the playoffs, 27-17.

Steve had a rough season as well. He injured a shoulder against Indianapolis on October 15, and a month later had minor arthroscopic surgery. Amazingly, he missed only five games. In his return against the Rams, he completed 21 of 32 passes for 226 yards and 3 touchdowns, as the Niners won, 41-13.

Despite missing five games, Steve wound up the season with more than 3,200 passing yards and 20 touchdowns. And the 49ers were the highest-scoring team in the league.

Still close to his parents and brothers, Steve has continued to live in Provo, Utah, during the off-season. He has never gone far from his Mormon roots. He has devoted a great deal of time to charity work through the Forever Young Foundation and other organizations, and has worked on behalf of children, the disabled, and Native Americans. He has campaigned vigorously against drug use.

On the field, Steve has overcome every roadblock in his way. First critics said he couldn't throw. He proved them wrong. Then they said he couldn't replace a college quarterback as good as Jim McMahon. He became a consensus All-American.

And finally, he had to play in the shadow of the greatest quarterback of them all — Joe Montana. No one can say that Steve has surpassed Joe. But he has certainly pulled up alongside him. Four straight passing titles, numerous records, two MVPs, and a Super Bowl victory. You can't ask for much more than that.

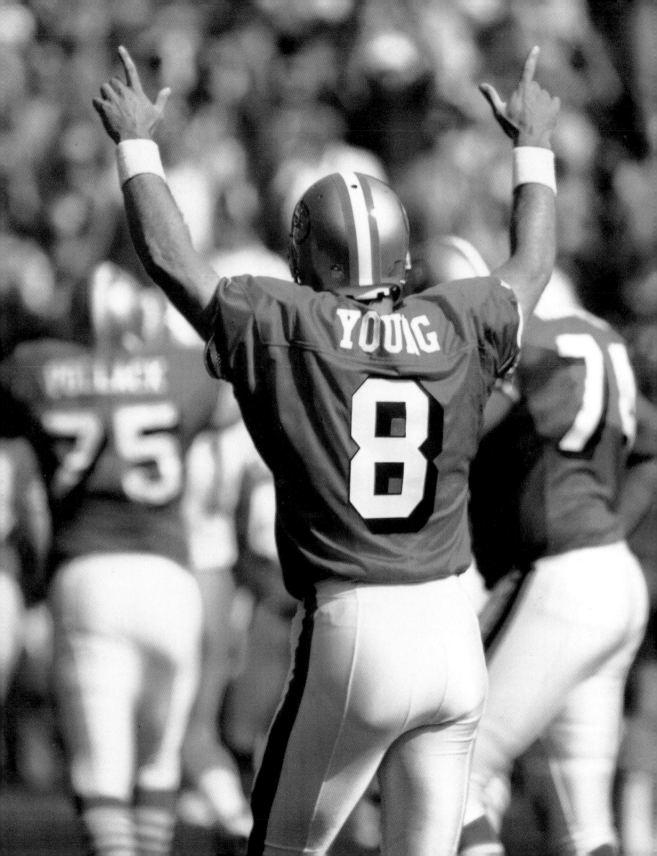

# STEVE YOUNG: HIGHLIGHTS

1961    Born on October 11 in Salt Lake City, Utah.

1982    Becomes the starting quarterback for the Brigham Young University Cougars.
Named Western Athletic Conference Offensive Player of the Year.

1983    Becomes consensus All-American.
Voted runner-up for the Heisman Trophy.
Leads the Cougars to an 11-1 season and a victory over Missouri in the Holiday Bowl.
Sets or ties 13 National Collegiate Athletic Association (NCAA) records.

1984    Signs with the Los Angeles Express of the now-defunct United States Football League (USFL).

1985    Signs a contract with the NFL Tampa Bay Buccaneers.

1987    Traded by the Buccaneers to the San Francisco 49ers.

1991    Replaces the injured Joe Montana as 49ers starting quarterback.

1992    Named the NFL's Most Valuable Player.

1993    Wins third straight NFL passing title.
Becomes the first 49er quarterback to throw for more than 4,000 yards in a season.

1994    Leads the 49ers to a league-best 13-3 record.
Sets an NFL all-time record with a quarterback rating of 112.8.
Named the NFL's Most Valuable Player for the second time.
Leads 49ers to a 49-26 Super Bowl victory over the San Diego Chargers, throwing a record six Super Bowl touchdowns.
Named the Most Valuable Player of Super Bowl XXIX.

1995    Despite missing five games to a shoulder injury, helps the 49ers to another divisional title (11-5) while throwing 20 touchdown passes.

# FIND OUT MORE

Bock, Hal. *Steve Young*. New York: Chelsea House, 1996.

Devaney, John. *Winners of the Heisman Trophy*. New York: Walker & Co., 1994.

Gutman, Bill. *Football*. North Bellmore, N.Y.: Marshall Cavendish, 1990.

Ruffo, Dave. *Football*. Austin, Tex.: Raintree Steck-Vaughn, 1993.

Weber, Bruce. *Pro-Football Megastars*. New York: Scholastic, 1994.

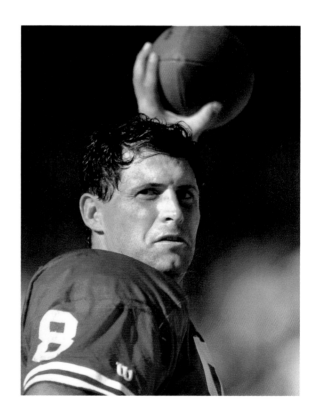

*How to write to Steve Young:*

Steve Young
c/o San Francisco 49ers
4949 Centennial Blvd.
Santa Clara, CA
95054-1229

# INDEX